Business Technology Trends For Beyond 2015

How to Use Online Technology In A Modern Workplace

By

Thomas Eriksson

eCare Publishing *Copyright* © 2015

Disclaimer

Table of Contents

Introduction

Reducing overhead costs is necessary in any business, but when you have a small business, it is imperative to keep costs low. Small business technology trends are commanding businesses to look at their efficiency, so they may compete on a more even playing field. Six areas can use an upgrade, or reformation in any business to utilize technology in a smarter, savvier way. How to use online technology in the modern workplace is about reducing bulky technology in-house, by utilizing the full offerings available in the cloud, upping your marketing game, finding CRMs and software to complement your business, including security necessities, and keeping up with predictions beyond 2015.

The business trends for beyond 2015 will help you streamline your company for a more effective future. Technology is always going to change and it is difficult to keep up with some aspects of these modifications due to the quickness with which technology is updated.

Desktop computers and laptops sold to you in bulk for an affordable cost may be obsolete in the next month. Many computers prior to the second quarter were still sold with Windows 8. Now Microsoft has released Windows 10. A computer bought in February 2015 is considered obsolete, at least as far as the operating system is concerned. Other areas of the new computer's technology can change just as quickly. A new model can be launched with an upgrade to the processor, keypad, screen size or amount and type of inputs. Keeping up with this expensive technology is difficult for any business; especially, small businesses with a smaller budget for technology. The current trends for small businesses is to look for ways you can stop spending as much on physical technology and still get the job done. Unless you continue to read and keep up with the changing trends in online technology, you will continue to be behind your competitors and struggle to keep your business moving forward in the next decade.

Chapter 1

Reducing Bulky Technology

Prior to 15 years ago, offices with a need for every employee to have a computer, meant a place filled with desktop units, printers, servers, network switches, and a great deal of other technology requirements. The cost of buying it all and then maintaining it over the long-term did not help a business' bottom line.

When desktop computers are obsolete months after they are purchased, there are still ways to maintain a semblance of structure. New software updates help a great deal with operating system changes, launches of new email and word processor programs, but even those updates can be expensive.

Just eight years ago, the standard for computer memory and hard drive space was 2GB of memory and 320GB of hard drive space. Today desktops are coming standard from the manufacturer with a minimum, 8GB of memory and a 1TB hard drive. There has also been a change in acceptable screen size, with a larger screen working better for employees due to the multiple applications needed to conduct their work. With social apps like Skype, and the necessity to speak with management across town, or an ocean away, outlook or other email software, and the ability to work in another window, the larger the screen, the easier it is to see everything going on.

Offices have been able to change since the advent of more affordable network installations, where printers with wireless capabilities have ensured a need for only one or two printers in a small business. Now every desk does not need to have its own printer.

Small businesses can also reduce the need for their own servers or costly server locations due to changes in technology.

For 2015 and beyond, the trend will continue to change the type of hardware necessary for a business to conduct its work. It is not worth the cost to maintain expensive IT equipment, upgrade systems, service contracts, or a fully IT infrastructure like it used to be.

The Forecast of Changes

Every business has its own needs. Call centers and in-house based businesses like accountant offices are going to retain their number of desktop computers or dual purpose tablets. Tablets that can be used as laptops are going to be more popular for a majority of businesses across a various industries. The reason is mobility and consumer satisfaction. Sometimes it can be easier for an office person to go to the client, versus bringing the client into their office.

It also requires fewer unsightly connections to remove the bulky excess of additional equipment and allows the consumer to opt for a streamlined technology that can work anywhere. Consider a mobile phone store, which uses tablets to check people in, and then the representative helping the consumer is able to go to them anywhere in the store. They sign in with the tablet, let the consumer see what they see, and make the changes or upgrades to a person's account.

Technology is not only becoming less bulky, but allowing employees and company representatives the option of being much more mobile. Instead of standing in one spot, which is hard on the feet, legs, and back—a company representative is getting exercise as they walk around helping consumers in an office setting.

Wireless technology cleans up the workplace and reduces potential electrical issues. Yes, the technology needs to be charged, but once it has been charged, the company representative can unplug the device. This saves energy. There are also fewer electrical outlets needed, with fewer wires to trip on, see or step over.

Mobility Required

Wireless technology not only enhances the look of your workspace, but it is a must for the younger generations. The newer generations are learning how to run business applications with nothing but a smartphone. Bosses and other staff are also going to own tablets and smartphones that make work easier. According to Laurie McCabe of SMB Group, "A growing majority of small businesses regard mobile solutions as essential business enables with 60% saying, mobile solutions are critical to business."

Mobile solutions are going to account for a larger share in the small business budget going forward, as they have already for the last four years.

Moving Towards Less

On the move towards less technology in the company, there is a direct link to utilizing the cloud. Greg Schulz is an analyst for Server and StorageIO Group, who believes getting rid of as much technology in-house as possible is the way to go in the future, because the cloud offers a better monetary and streamlined choice.

The Cloud structure requires less IT technology in the building from network switches to cords running through the floor, in the ceiling, or along the edge of the walls. Once the equipment is reduced in a business, which lowers the overhead spent on a yearly basis, companies have time to focus on more important aspects of their business and utilize those funds elsewhere.

Chapter 2

Going to the Cloud

The Cloud or cloud computing is the future for any business; especially, small businesses that need to lower their overhead costs and streamline their technology in-house. Through the use of the Cloud, businesses are able to reduce their bulky technology.

Overview of the Cloud

The Cloud or cloud computing, refers to storage solutions for any computer user, where data is stored and processed by a third-party data center. There is an infrastructure, platform, and application level to the Cloud. You can think of the Cloud as an electricity grid. It can handle multiple levels all in one little cloud. Several people can access the Cloud through tablets, phones, laptops, servers, and desktops. They can pull from storage, an object storage, monitor certain aspects of business and collaborate on projects.

The collaboration and storage options are really where small businesses will benefit. You no longer need a huge backup system complete with at least one computer that acts like a server in your office building.

You can upload all the files you want saved directly to the cloud, where it gets stored in a massive third-party storage server. While you are going to reduce the amount of storage you have on site, you still want a backup system. The main idea is to have a smaller hard drive to backup to because you only need to keep certain files on hand at all times.

Increasing Backup and Recovery in the Cloud

For 2015 and beyond, more businesses are going to increase their backup and recovery to the cloud. The internal expense of keeping it in-house is too high, according to analysts at Ptak Associates. Small businesses are looking to streamline their storage and recovery solutions, which means going to the cloud for data backup, data recovery, disaster recovery, and data archiving.

Do you have files from eight years ago on the same computer hard drive? Most businesses do. They want to have their files backed up to the server, as well as have a secondary place to back up their files. With cloud storage options, you can send all but the last year and current year to the Cloud. It will still be available through regular access, in a data backup, plus there will be disaster recovery protocols the Cloud operator is responsible for. This gives your employees and you more time to focus on saving the files, letting it upload and backup automatically to the Cloud, and continue with the more important work in the office.

There are two considerations to make when considering using the Cloud for backup and recovery. Off-premises services are going to have a cost depending on how rapidly you want to get to your data when a recovery situation arises.

Always check on the price and the rapid recovery options the company can offer. There are free services out there. These freeware services like Dropbox and OneDrive are setup more for personal user use, rather than a small or large business. The freeware options are there for recovery, but it is usually a slow process.

You don't have to pay huge amounts to get a reputable service with a decent disaster recovery time. However, you should not rely solely on the Cloud for your recovery either. According to Mike Karp, of Ptak Associates, you want to have the Cloud for safeguarding your files, but not rely on it completely. You still want to have the files you would need should a disaster occur. A local copy helps you move quicker.

Starting New Projects

Going forward, more businesses are going to start new projects from their Cloud service. The Cloud offers mobility, IT functions, and the ability to analyze customer databases. It will not matter whether you are going to create a new mobile or social app, rebuild an internal system, or any other business project. The Cloud's options for starting new projects and accessing ongoing projects are a time saver.

Perhaps you have in-house employees, but also some telecommuters. Your telecommuters can pull data from the Cloud with regards to a project, while the in-house employees are also updating other portions of the project. Since everyone is linked to the same account, the updates will show up giving employees the knowledge of when a project has been updated and may be available for viewing.

If you need to have a meeting with multiple employees, they can all be at their desks, looking at the same projects and following along on social platforms like a Skype conference.

Some businesses need to hire writers, and rather than sending an email, the writer can access the information directly from the cloud, download the proper file, and upload the work when it is done.

The Cloud is here to stay and it is the best option for starting new projects that need to be viewed by multiple people. For the above reasons, analysts believe the Cloud is going to become the place to save projects, data, and recover data.

Data Archiving

Before ending the conversation on the Cloud, there is one more important point to make for businesses going forward. Many businesses have certain legal requirements regarding documents and data that need to be generated, received, or kept. Storage, such as backup drives for computers, is getting more affordable. Yet, you may find you do not need to keep every file, piece of paper, or document you have ever created. With computer backup systems and the Cloud, you can be selective in what you store and where. Any data you have that adds value to your business needs to be protected, stored, and treated like a business asset, according to key analysts.

You will want to break down your data into sections based on the level of importance. If you do not need access to it all the time and want to purchase affordable storage you can do so. If you need access, but do not need it taking up space within the company, then storing it in the cloud is wise—you can always have security on those files that limit access to just you and other key individuals. Lastly, you can use the Cloud to create accessible files that are used daily, such as new projects. You always want to have sensible data archiving to make it easier to find key pieces of information or documents.

Chapter 3

Marketing Protocols

Marketing is the reason most new businesses, particularly small businesses, fail within the first two years of opening. Small businesses with small budgets do not have the proper marketing techniques on their side to ensure their company is able to survive in the competitive world. Companies with innovative and successful marketing practices, are going to survive beyond the two year mark, and even beyond the ten year mark. The trend has been changing with ever increasing technological advancements. Bigger companies competing with smaller companies, are using highly sophisticated marketing techniques, which helps attract consumers.

If small businesses want to stay with the trend and remain competitive with other businesses, they need to increase their game. Cloud based marketing options are making it possible for smaller business to market at lower costs.

Laurie McCabe says the "right automated marketing tools," is an imperative decision for any business to make. Several vendors offer usable, solid, and valuable marketing approaches that small businesses can use. Certainly, there is no one solution for all businesses; however, after thorough research it is possible to find the marketing solution that fits your company. McCabe states a business owner or operator needs to "develop a short list that includes solutions that offer the capabilities and services you need, as well as integration with other solutions your business requires."

Creating a list of what marketing your business needs will help you get through the hype that vendors use. The internet is filled with marketing techniques that are meant to be cost effective solutions and yet many of them eat away at your time. Just going with the hype that vendors are pedaling is not the right solution. It takes going to an on-site event or utilizing a webinar to see the automated marketing tools. Any company looking for marketing tools should use the free trials offered.

Word of mouth references from other businesses you trust and that are similar to your company, are also helpful to finding the proper marketing tools. You can learn about their experiences implementing, using, and obtaining value from the automated marketing tools another company has.

Test driving more than one marketing solution is imperative as a way to learn how it works and what is going to work best for your company. With all types of marketing and with the trend heading towards cloud based tools, there are just too many to list here for the various business models out there. This is why reading up on marketing solutions, and using free trials, as well as asking for references will be the best way for you to locate the solution you need.

Marketing Trend 2: Integrated Marketing

Along with finding automated marketing solutions for your business, the small business trend has been to integrate marketing. Software Advice conducted a study with the result that US small businesses are realizing the importance of consumer connections throughout the buying cycle (Software Advice is a company that helps find the right software for buyers). With the need to keep in touch with the buyer throughout their buying cycle, companies are looking towards marketing functions with integrated sales. It means companies are utilizing Customer Relationship Marketing suites. The following chapter will explain more about the functionality of the CRMs, but for now, understand the trend Software Advice has found is that 62% of small businesses are buying CRMs, with basic contact management.

Businesses want a standalone application for SFA (sales force automation). It should not be surprising that SFA requirements are the first area small businesses look to with regard to tracking consumer data and consumer interactions within the company or website.

Software Advice also found that 42% of US companies want an integrated CRM with multiple applications, rather than a standalone SFA option that has basic marketing automation or customer service options. According to Jay Ivey, of Software Advice, "the number has jumped from 7% in 2013 to 42%". In just a year more companies have stopped searching for standalone SFAs and started looking for a full CRM suite.

US companies looking for the integrated marketing software has jumped to 88%, based on a combination of marketing and sales automation. Software Advice's bottom line, according to the article is that "more small businesses want fuller-featured CRMs to better align marketing and sales." According to the author of Small Business Computing's article *10 Small Business Technology Trends*, 71% of businesses want cloud based CRM systems versus in-house systems. The ratio has increased from 2013, when it was only 48% two years ago.

The trend is fairly clear for any small business looking at their current marketing and sales strategies. It is necessary to find automated marketing tools, while maintaining the tracking ability on sales. The more functions a program provides, the more tracking the business can conduct to target their consumers and increase their sales. Furthermore, with the trend towards cloud computing solutions, companies want to streamline their business software in all areas of the company.

Marketing is taking on New Forms

Andrew Stanten wrote *5 Marketing Trends You Can't Afford to Ignore in 2015*, where he discusses the latest trends in gaining market share. For small companies hoping to get a piece of the action against larger corporations or to simply be above the competition, there are always going to be changing marketing trends. Stanten has five that may be extremely important to your small business.

"Always-on advertising" is about "inference advertising" where you need to target consumers based on their devices. The one thing most people are going to be looking at daily is their smart phone or mobile device connected to the internet. Not only is the company supposed to target the device that is always in use, but there are some smart ways to integrate technology within those devices. Take a minute to consider your smoke detector. What if your smoke detector's alarm sounded and the next day you received an email to help with smoke damage cleanup. You might not need the offer for the simple kitchen smoke that occurred, but the company is in tune with your need.

Any small business can infer what a consumer might require, hence the always-on advertising. Using media like emails and online advertisements, you can follow the trend of competitors to target your consumers.

You already gain information when a consumer stops by your website or store. You know through marketing software and CRM systems what a person bought, how long they spent online finding the product and what else they may have looked at. The trend for beyond 2015 is for smaller businesses to pay more attention to these details.

A consumer may have purchased soap from a local soap maker. The soap is designed to last for three months with the person washing every day. With inference advertising, the person will receive an email a week before the three month deadline. As a discount coupon email, it entices the consumer back to the store, providing they liked the product of course.

Another trend is being able to wear devices. Apple is coming out with the watch with phone capabilities, which is designed to outdo all other products of a similar nature. Now someone can be on their smartphone without it being in their hand. Starbucks created a smartphone platform for paying with gift cards, earning rewards, and now being able to tip the barista. Any small business can come up with an app or "wearable" concept that will make their consumer think about them.

Three other tips include using mobile web browsing to your advantage, using better online content, and using resources in a better way. The trend for the last three years has been moving towards mobile devices. Now classrooms are gaining mobile technology and allowing children to bring their tablets for better learning. It all means that a small business must have a website, and marketing in place for that website to be found, according to Stanten.

There is a small issue with content and websites due to a trend of increasing consumer disbelief. Everyone knows there have been issues with online content generation. Certain websites offering information have a bad reputation because of their rocky start. Yet, you cannot avoid posting and updating your website content on a regular basis. You also need to have ads constantly changed to fit the consumer trends. All it takes is a few extra seconds to look over the marketing blog, advertisement, or content to ensure it is the best it can be and backed with expert sources. Without it, the marketing ploy will fail, hence the trend to find better writers rather than going it alone even in small businesses.

A lot of the trends so far have discussed technology, streamlining your processes, and utilizing services that will help you. It is the more intelligent resource allocation you can do in your business. It also applies to market as it does to the technology you have in your company. You may find a larger advertising budget with reduced overhead, but you need to make certain it is going to the right place.

The focus needs to be on advertising in the right places, on mobile platforms, and the generation of new content. You cannot blast out advertisements and hope it will work. You need to use advertisements to generate targeted consumer interest. Following these tips and trends, will also enable you to use systems such as integrated marketing CRMs.

Chapter 4

CRMs and Software for Streamlined Working

Software Advice makes it clear that CRM systems and software that will benefit the company is necessary for streamlining business processes and succeeding in targeted marketing plans (Robb, 2015). In order to find the correct CRM software, companies may want to look at additional trends such as small businesses, avoiding the social technology that is unnecessary for their CRM software.

According to the research, social technology has been beneficial for a select few small businesses. A blog that helps bring in new clientele or a Facebook page that gains thousands of followers has been useful; however, it does not work for every company. Most small businesses that try to use social media for their marketing will not see the return they desire. The reason that social media marketing is not as successful as one hopes, is that it is unnecessary to have it integrated into the CRM application. Some software has social media channels attached, but this social functionality can be too bulky for what a company truly requires.

Ivey stated, "Rather than social functionality, we found that most buyers request basic CRM integration with popular email clients." The article further states Microsoft Outlook or Gmail is desired about 58%, while calendar apps like Apple's iCloud or Google's Calendar are desired 36% of the time. These two applications will help synchronize employees so that all follow-up reminders, meetings, tasks, and other responsibilities are the focus of the employee, whether they are logging into the CRM system each day or not.

From the research mentioned in *10 Small Business Technology Trends for 2015,* combined with research by individuals like Ivey—it is clear that the trend is heading toward CRM with cloud based applications.

Social Media Marketing Trends

In the last six years a trend towards using social media has blossomed. It started with Facebook, viral videos, and Twitter. Blogs that went viral also caught the attention of many small businesses. Several authoritative websites started telling small business owners that social media is a must for marketing. The "free marketing" trend also began with many articles filling the web stating that if you use social media in your small business you save money on marketing. But, more recently studies have started showing that social media marketing and its "free" attributes are not all they are cracked up to be. Peter Visser wrote *Why Social Media Marketing Does Not Work for Small Businesses* two years ago (2013). Now there are thousands of articles stating similar reasons for why social media marketing is not an essential part of a small business' marketing arsenal.

The article is not saying social media should be ignored, but rather that it shouldn't be relied on solely for marketing a small business. Small businesses need to use their time to create more sales and focus on important aspects of business. However, they also need to have a variety of marketing options in place. Marketing that targets specific consumers to make a sale is a better use of an employee's time in a small business over keeping up with social media pages like Facebook.

Take a moment to see how the trend has actually worked. Try to find business Facebook pages for small companies in your area. Actually, look up your competitors in your area and in other states. Approximately 70% of the time you will see a Facebook page that started two to four years ago, and you know this because the posts started out strong with multiple posts in the first year and then the Facebook page started to taper off with fewer posts as time progressed. For those that started longer than two years ago, you will probably see that about two years ago was the last post made to that page. The small business found it was no longer viable to use social media.

Consistency is key to any social media campaign, as well as having valuable content and not just another short post.

Another article on social media by Kirill Kniazev was written more recently. Kniazev published *Social Media is not Enough: Why Every Small Business Needs a (Good) Website* in July 2015. The main point of this article is to state that social media is not where most consumers are going to search for products, services or to shop. When someone sits down at the computer to look at their emails or social media pages, it is to get up to date with the current events in their social lives. They are not going to these pages to find a new product. The mentality of visiting social media pages is different. The mind is set on spending a few hours catching up with friends and enjoying a few games.

Small businesses need that mind set to be focused on purchases. Marketing in places that the consumer has gone specifically for shopping is going to generate more sales.

This is where the CRMs come in handy. With automated marketing and sales systems, a small business is going to target the consumer at the time the consumer is on and where they are online. Marketing can be done in the middle of the night to get the night owls or the people just getting off of work, while the small business is closed. The other lesson, which is showing up in marketing and CRM usage trends is that SEO is still the king of marketing a website, products, and services for small companies.

Consumers are going to use a search engine, word of mouth, or referral to a website over social media.

Software to Level the Competition

Before the Cloud most software was labelled as "small business" or "enterprise" to differentiate between the sizes of a company the software product was written for. Now vendors are writing software for the Cloud, enabling it to be a user-based pricing system. Software that was once for larger businesses and only affordable by such companies for on-premises use, has a price structure for the Cloud. Smaller companies are able to buy a single use license for their company and use the same software larger enterprises are using.

Vendors are going to continue this trend. The vendor gets to sell more software to more companies. They also get to target functional areas of businesses no matter the size. It will not make a one-size-fits all product, but according to Chris Neuman from DataHero, it will help to level the competition with regards to usable software.

Small companies can pay a smaller price point to access software that is working for larger businesses and that will work for their companies as well.

Smaller businesses are definitely getting the advantage with this trend that will remain well past the 2015 mark. More availability in software choices combined with the Cloud, leads to the necessity of protecting it all with more than just the programs written into the software.

Chapter 5

Security Necessities

Running any business requires certain security to be in place from who is allowed to see certain documents, to ensuring the competition is not learning any company secrets. The Cloud provides a new way to consider security in any business given the breaches in security that can occur. With the trend of utilizing the Cloud increasing, businesses will see fewer costs and more functionality; however, it also opens the potential of an outsider gaining business information. The business size is not going to stop hackers and malicious individuals from getting in to a company's secure data; particularly, if there is an opening. Many people who attempt to get through a company's security do it for the challenge. If there is a "new" security, like the chip and pin system on credit cards, you know there are people trying to crack it to prove that nothing is safe from an outside attack.

Any business, whether it is wholly dependent on technology or not, needs to pay more attention to computer security. Analysts also believe that a "technology-centric" system is not the answer (Robb, 2015). It takes more than just technology to keep a company safe.

Standard Security

Technology based security systems are antivirus and antispam software. There are several options sold in the market and quite a few that are free with certain restrictions. Microsoft has their own free program in the form of Microsoft Security Essentials for older systems and Windows Defender for the latest operating system. Whether you buy your program or use a free one, they can only do so much. Most have spyware and viruses that unsavory individuals have created in order to get a back door into any computer that uses them.

If you read through various computer tech magazines you will learn even more about the ability of hackers to get through security codes. Even the top businesses have suffered from viruses and spyware. A few years ago, the Army had trouble with a virus, which meant all computers using their software had to be checked, fixed, and in some cases completely removed from the military network to avoid any further issues.

You have companies that hire security specialists, with computer geniuses that have hacked the best computer security systems in the world in order to avoid attacks. For small businesses this is not a reasonable option. Most small businesses buy a program, hope it will work, and focus on the important day to day running of their company.

Experts state that for every new program, there are at least half a dozen individuals trying to crack that new security program, the update, or the patch to fix an old security breach. It can take a matter of months for the new update or security patch to be breached again or a few years, but it will happen. For every intelligent individual building these programs, there are just as many individuals breaking them.

The ease with which some businesses are broken into via technological security breaches, leads to the necessity of having increased security awareness in your company.

Employee Security Awareness

Technology is just one way to make your company secure. Security awareness training is a must in any business and where most companies fail to pay attention.

Businesses will publish their policies regarding internet and computer usage. These policies typically include security procedures, as well as an overview of the technologies in place to ensure the company's data is safe.

According to Stu Sjouwerman, CEO of KnowBe4, businesses need to focus on training their employees in conjunction with technology. Mr. Sjouwerman believes training is the most important aspect of security for the new cloud technology and world that businesses operate in. By putting employees through security awareness training, it helps to make staff members understand the avenues of attack, scammers and hackers use.

Many of the scams focused on businesses start with a clickable link or document in an email. It gives the hacker access to the company data as soon as the click has occurred to either download the document or follow the link.

Worse, these links or documents appear legitimate. Unless employees are hyper aware of how these hackers work it is difficult to eliminate the human element as the vulnerable opening into a company.

A few slides during a lunch or meeting are not enough, according to Mr. Sjouwerman. Rather, he believes it takes regular, repetitive training with simulation. Sjouwerman's company begins with organized attacks via email. They look to see how many employees will open the email then click on the attachment or link. He then educates the employees in the company showing them the tricks that are used by nefarious individuals trying to steal company information through security breaches. After the training, Sjouwerman's company fakes attacks yet again. A few weeks of training and fake attacks usually leads to a lower number of employees clicking on things they should not. The number will never be zero.

Since the number of employees will never be zero, regarding those who avoid clicking on links and downloading documents they should not, it is imperative for the company to be vigilant in their training.

The number one rule, according to Mr. Sjouwerman, is to "think before you click."

Security awareness training is honing the point that employees have to do their part, think rather than just click, and lower the potential threat. In a smaller company it can be easier to keep an eye on employees, but you have more important tasks as the owner or manager. By providing frequent training, education, and monitoring the employees, it will be easier to keep your employees on their toes.

Parental Controls

Setting up a secure system is necessary, particularly with the use of cloud computing. It is possible to set up computers on your network for specific users and have an administrative access account that locks out all other employees.

A network administrator setting with a pin or password is one way to keep employees from changing "parental controls." The business network requires a different set of controls that lock out your employees, but you can consider yourself the administrator with parental controls. You can eliminate the potential of visiting certain websites. Any website you block is a website your employee cannot access.

Unless you use an email other than outlook for your email system, go ahead and lock Gmail, Yahoo, and other personal email systems. By blocking access to these email locations, there is less chance that an employee will use your computer to access their private email and potentially open up a spam email filled with a virus or spyware.

What to Allow

As a company owner or operator, you have to decide what is allowed by the employee. If you intend on using the Cloud for your business, you do have to make certain the service you use is secure. You can choose to allow the Cloud service, your email service, and access by certain employees to your website.

When you use the Cloud, there is a potential for a document to get into your server from the service you use. It is another reason that using security awareness will help you lower the risk should a wrong file get uploaded. By teaching your employees about files and the ability to carry a virus or spyware, you can also ensure that your employee will tell you about files they do not recognize. For example, a file that was not there yesterday and is not saved according to the company format.

Taking Security up another Notch

How you save files in the Cloud is as important as the security protocols you have in place. As the trend towards security awareness training picks up in the next few years and the use of the Cloud is also increasing, you have to have a system for saving files.

A saved file from your company should have a protocol that is followed. It may be the client name, project start date, and a code you reference. In fact, the system should be something a hacker would not know unless they were within the company or associated with an employee of the company. The idea is to create a code filing system that will look correct to your employees—without being something a hacker can figure out.

This saves your employees from looking at files and thinking they do not belong because the code you use will immediately tell them a new file is correct. It helps separate out the files that do not belong too, ensuring you hear about any file in the Cloud that could accidentally be opened to a back door.

Chapter 6

Technology Predictions Beyond 2015

The trends do not stop with cloud based computer technology. Gartner recently published an article detailing 10 strategic technology predictions for the coming years. These trends will examine how machines and humans will interact not only in business, but in everyday life.

Daryl Plummer, the vice president and Gartner Fellow, believes machines are going to have more humanistic qualities in order to personalize the relationship between the machine and the human. This means the current trends and predicted trends will pair humans and machines as "co-workers or codependents," versus a machine that aids in the humans employment.

If you are thinking the coming trends are more about systems like Microsoft's Windows 10 you are right. Already the example is here for where the future is endeavoring to go. Windows 10 is paired with Cortana enabling any machines running the system to utilize the Windows search engine by voice or by typing. It is tied to Internet Explorer at the moment, so some individuals may avoid it rather than use it, but overall the next wave is already here.

With concepts like Cortana, an employee can do a quick search for information on the web or from within windows. It means if the employee needs to find a file in the Cloud, the automated software called Cortana will be able to find it, open it, and let the employee work on it.

Another trend that has steadily increased in its technological advancements is voice commands. Word processors are able to work with voice systems, allowing an employee to speak instead of type. The technology is not quite perfected—yet. There is still a learning curve for operator and machine. It takes hours for the machine to learn how the person speaks to avoid typing errors. There is also an issue with the microphone being used for the voice commands. A sub-par microphone will hinder the speech patterns a person makes and thus the technology is limited in what it "hears."

Despite current drawbacks, the trend is certainly going towards a more automated and voice commanded world over typing. For example, the future of a doctor's office is for the system to take the voice commands of the doctor and input the information into the computer system. Doctors will no longer need to pause to type notes, send off prescription requests and print out information. It will all be available through the Cloud and computer voice commands. Since this technology is already here, it benefits a small business to learn about the technology that will continue to take corporations and employees to the next level.

Gartner has 10 predictions that a small business should know about:

- At the end of 2016, it is projected that $2 billion in online sales will be through "mobile digital assistants." These assistants will do all the work rather than having an employee handle online sales. Programs will have a more hands on approach to filling orders than they already do, at least in some businesses. For smaller companies digital assistants can only take the work to a certain point.

- In 2017, mobile sales is also expected to drive mobile revenue up by 50% in the US. Gartner explains it is an increase in Apple Pay, Google Wallet, and other NFC technology being used to make purchases versus credit cards and electronic systems like PayPal.

- The year 2017 will mark a "disruptive digital business" launch, where the business model is based on a computer algorithm. It will change how "physical logistics" form the "business ecosystem."

- 2017 will also mark a shift in consumer needs, where 70% "of successful digital business models will rely on" hyper maneuverable systems to create a competitive business advantage. The new business model is unstable, but will allow the business to move with the customer needs in order to keep up with the competition companies are working against.

- Companies will use 50% of their "consumer product investments" to create innovations for consumer experiences. In simple terms, consumer products currently bought in stores like CDs, movies, and other similar products, will have digital extensions rather than being traditional products.

- Additionally by 2017, online retailers will start using 3D printing to create personalized products for consumers. About 20% will convert to making their own products with 3D printing versus buying from drop shippers or manufacturers. The end result is a better bottom line for the online retailer.

- By 2018, businesses are going to need 50% fewer employees that process data, but there will be a need for 500% more digital business related jobs versus the traditional models existing right now.

- Another 2018 prediction is the cost of business operations will decrease by 30% due to smart machines and more "industrialized services" (Spender, 2015).

- Retail businesses will integrate targeted messaging along with an internal positioning system (IPS) by 2020. This system will increase sales by as much as 5%. It also means businesses will increase the offers they have for consumers based on location and the time they spent in the physical store.

In assessing the trends, it is clear that there are many changes coming starting now and going into 2020. Each year as technology continues to change and improve there will be new predictions and possibly changes to this current list. However, as a business owner or operator, it is important for you to know where everything is headed and what changes are mostly going to affect your type of business. Every company has their own business model and needs with regards to technology, even an automotive shop.

Certain technology trends will work for specific types of companies like retailers and it won't work for others.

Tech Trends Survey

Tech Trends releases a survey by Accenture. The survey polled 2,000 business and technology executives in nine countries and 10 different industries (Accenture, 2015). The survey shows 62% of businesses are investing in digital technology, and 35% are investing in digital concepts for their business strategy. With the trend in digital technology these businesses are able to incorporate all aspects of business, customer relationships, and the world surrounding them. For larger businesses, these companies are touching billions of lives through digital technology. For small businesses the trend is increasing, enabling the smaller companies to touch more lives than just in their immediate area.

The trend is showing companies can see the connections beyond customers and employees. They are seeing a global network of individuals, businesses, and things from around the world in various industries. This creates the "digital ecosystems" mentioned by Gartner. The grand ability to connect through transforming business models is increasing sales for companies.

The survey also states that 81% of those polled believe that industry boundaries are going to become blurred due to the reshaping of platforms based on the business ecosystems. Digital technology is going to provide a higher efficiency for most businesses small or large.

The key to these trends mentioned in the survey is how well you keep up with the information as it is released. Companies that use their digital relationships with consumers, end users, alliance partners, suppliers, developers, data sources, specialty talent, and makers of various smart devices will succeed over businesses that do not keep up to date.

As long as you are willing to keep up with the trends and be a company that starts a few new trends, you will survive in the digital ecosystems that are being generated even as this book is written. Companies are able to determine their own fortunes and there are opportunities and trends you do not want to miss.

Conclusion

Thank you again for purchasing this book!

We hope this book was able to help you in your needs and to satisfy your reading pleasures.

Finally, if you enjoyed this book, please take the time to share your thoughts and post a review on Amazon. It would be greatly appreciated!

Thank you and good luck!

Check Out My Other Books

Please feel free to visit www.ecarepublishing.com to discover other books we have available.

We would be honored if you participated in our email notifications where you can get early bird announcements of our new upcoming books.

References

Accenture. (2015). *Digital business Era: Stretch Your Boundaries*. Retrieved from Tech Trends: http://techtrends.accenture.com/us-en/business-technology-trends-report.html

Knaizev, K. (2015, July 8). *Social Media is Not Enough: Why Small Business Needs a (Good) Website*. Retrieved from Business 2 Community: http://www.business2community.com/small-business/social-media-not-enough-every-small-business-needs-good-website-01270481

Robb, D. (2015, January 7). *10 Small Business Technology Trends for 2015*. Retrieved from Small Business COmputing: http://www.smallbusinesscomputing.com/biztools/10-small-business-technology-trends-for-2015.html

Spender, A. (2015, February 18). *Top 10 Strategic Technology Predictions for 2015 and Beyond*. Retrieved from Gartner: http://www.gartner.com/smarterwithgartner/top-10-strategic-technology-predictions-for-2015-and-beyond/

Stanten, A. (2015). *5 Marketing Trends You Can't Afford to Ignore in 2015*. Retrieved from Altitude Marketing: http://altitudemarketing.com/5-marketing-trends-cant-afford-ignore-2015/

Visser, P. (2013). *Why Social Media Marketing Does Not Work for Small Businesses*. Retrieved from Big Mouth Marketing: http://bigmouthmarketing.co/why-social-media-marketing-does-not-work-for-small-businesses/

www.ingramcontent.com/pod-product-compliance
Lightning Source LLC
Chambersburg PA
CBHW071015180526
45168CB00003B/1425